Contents

» Any words appearing in bold, **like this,** are explained in the glossary.

Starting your science investigation

A science investigation is an exciting challenge. It starts with an idea that you can test by doing experiments. These are often lots of fun to do. But it is no good just charging in without planning first. A good scientist knows that they must first research their idea thoroughly, work out how they can test it, and plan their experiments carefully. When they have done these things, they can happily carry out their experiments to see if their idea is right.

Your experiments might support your original idea or they might shoot it down in flames. This doesn't matter. The important thing is that you will have found out a bit more about the world around you, and had fun along the way. You will be a happy scientist!

An **ecosystem** is all the living and non-living things interacting with one another in a certain area. In this book, you'll look at nine science investigations involving ecosystems. You'll discover some wonderful things about the world you live in.

Do your research

Is there something about ecosystems you've always wondered about? Something you don't quite understand but would like to? Then do a little research about the subject. Go to the library and find some books about the subject. Books written for students are often a very good place to start.

Use your favourite Internet search engine to find reliable online resources. Websites written by museums, universities, newspapers, and scientific journals are among the best sources for accurate research. Each investigation in this book has some suggestions for further research.

You need to make sure that your resources are reliable when doing research. Ask yourself the following questions, especially about the resources you find online.

The investigations

Background information

The start of each investigation contains a box like this.

Possible question

This question is a suggested starting point for your investigation. You will need to adapt the question to suit the things that interest you.

Possible hypothesis

This is only a suggestion. Don't worry if your hypothesis doesn't match the one listed here. Use your imagination!

Approximate cost of materials

Discuss this with your parents before starting work. Don't spend too much.

Materials needed

Make sure you can easily get all of the materials listed and gather them together before starting work.

Level of difficulty

There are three levels of investigations in this book: Easy, Intermediate, and Advanced. The level of difficulty is based on how long the investigation takes and how complicated it is.

1) How old is the resource? Is the information up to date or is it very old?

2) Who wrote the resource? Is the author identified so you know who they are, and what qualifies them to write about the topic?

3) What is the purpose of the resource? A website from a business or pressure group might not give balanced information, but one from a university probably will.

4) Is the information well documented? Can you tell where the author got their information from so you can check how accurate it is?

Some websites allow you to "chat" online with experts. Make sure you discuss this with a parent or teacher first. Never give out personal information online. The "Think U Know" website at http://www.thinkuknow.co.uk has loads of tips about safety online.

Once you know a little more about the subject you want to investigate, you'll be ready to work out your scientific question. You will be able to use this to make a sensible **hypothesis**. A hypothesis is an idea about why something happens that can be tested by doing experiments. Finally, you'll be ready to begin your science investigation!

What is an experiment?

Often when someone says that they are going to do an experiment, they mean they are just going to fiddle with something to see what happens. But scientists mean something else. They mean that they are going to control the **variables** involved in a careful way. A variable is something that changes or can be changed. Independent variables are things that you deliberately keep the same or change in your experiment. You should always aim to keep all the independent variables constant, except for the one you are investigating. The dependent variable is the change that happens because of the one independent variable that you do change. You make a fair test if you set up your experiment so that you only change one independent variable at a time. Your results are valid if you have carried out a fair test, and recorded your results or observations honestly.

You might want to compare one group with another to see what happens. For example, imagine you wanted to test whether fertiliser really helps grass grow. You might use six cups of grass seed. You would give three of them only water (Group A) and three of them liquid fertiliser (Group B). Group A is your **control** group and group B is your test group. You would be looking to see if there is a difference between the two groups. In this experiment, the liquid fertiliser is the independent variable, and the growth rate of the grass seed is the dependent variable.

You must do experiments carefully so that your results are accurate and reliable. Ideally, you would get the same results if you did your investigation all over again.

Your hypothesis

Once you've decided on the question you're going to try to answer, you then make a scientific **prediction** of what you'll find out in your science project.

For example, if you wonder what effect acid rain has on plant growth, your question might be, "Does acid affect plant growth?" Remember, a hypothesis is an idea about why something happens, which can be tested by doing experiments. So your hypothesis in response to the above question might be, "The amount of acid will affect plant growth." With a hypothesis, you can also work out if you can actually do the experiments needed to answer your question. Think of a question like: "What one factor changes an ecosystem?" It would be impossible to support your hypothesis, however you express it. So, be sure you can actually get the **evidence** needed to support or disprove your hypothesis.

Keeping records

Good scientists keep careful notes in their lab book about everything they do. This is really important. Other scientists may want to try out the experiments to see if they get the same results. So the records in your lab book need to be clear and easy to follow. What sort of things should you write down?

It is a good idea to write some notes about the research you found in books and on websites. You should also include the names of the books or the web addresses. This will save you from having to find these useful resources all over again later. You should also write down your hypothesis and your reasons for it. All your **data** and results should go into your lab book, too.

Your results are the evidence that you use to make your conclusion. Never rub out an odd-looking result or tweak it to "look right". An odd result may turn out to be important later. You should write down *every* result you get. Tables are a really good way to record lots of results clearly. Make sure you record when you did your experiments, and anything you might have changed along the way to improve them. No detail is too small when it comes to scientific research.

There are tips for making a great report with each investigation and at the end of this book. Use them as guides and don't be afraid to be creative. Make it *your* investigation!

My personal ecosystem

Did you know that there are many different ecosystems near your home or school? An ecosystem doesn't have to be huge. It could be as small as your garden – or even smaller, such as the area around a tree. In this experiment, you will choose one ecosystem to observe over time.

Do your research

For this project, you will note changes to **biotic** factors. These are living things, such as plants and animals. You may also notice changes to **abiotic** factors – non-living things, such as rocks and water. Research the plants, trees, and animals that live in the ecosystem you are studying. Don't forget to learn about the insects and other small creatures that also play an important role in any ecosystem. Then you'll be ready to begin this project or come up with your own.

You could start your research using this book and these websites:

» *Earth Science: Ecosystems and Biomes*, Barbara Davis (Gareth Stevens, 2007)
» What's the system? http://www.realtrees4kids.org/ninetwelve/system.htm
» Tree ecosystem: http://www.bbc.co.uk/schools/gcsebitesize/biology/ livingthingsenvironment/0habitatsandpopsrev5.shtml

Background information

Possible question

Will my ecosystem change over time?

Possible hypothesis

Both living and non-living things in my ecosystem will change.

Level of difficulty

Intermediate

Approximate cost of materials

£5.00

Materials needed

» Coloured pencils or other drawing materials, or camera and film or digital camera
» Outdoor thermometer (available at most hardware shops)
» Magnifying glass or binoculars for observing small plants and animals (optional)

Outline of methods

1. Choose an area that you will be able to observe frequently, such as your garden or an area around your school. It should be a place with at least one tree and some other plants.

Observing ants and other small creatures can help you understand an ecosystem.

Continued

2. Write the date and time in your lab book. Then make a detailed drawing or take a picture showing the different plants and animals you see. Label each photo or drawing. Make sure you look closely at the ground for insects and signs of animals, such as droppings, chewed leaves or nuts, burrows, even footprints. Look back at your sources or in field guides to help you identify any unknown plants or creatures.

Step 2

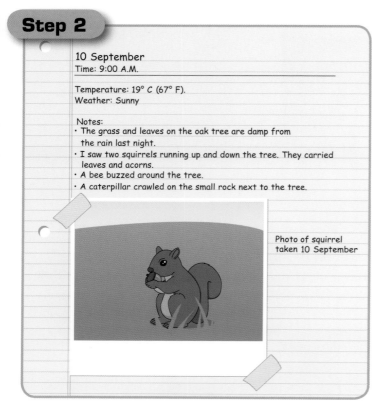

10 September
Time: 9:00 A.M.

Temperature: 19° C (67° F).
Weather: Sunny

Notes:
• The grass and leaves on the oak tree are damp from the rain last night.
• I saw two squirrels running up and down the tree. They carried leaves and acorns.
• A bee buzzed around the tree.
• A caterpillar crawled on the small rock next to the tree.

Photo of squirrel taken 10 September

3. Choose specific factors to look for each day, such as the number of leaves on the ground or how many ants you count. Note this data in your lab book. Also record the temperature and weather conditions – is it rainy, sunny, or cloudy?

4. The next day, observe your ecosystem again, looking for the same factors you observed the day before.

5. Continue to observe your ecosystem and note any changes for two weeks.

More activities to extend your investigation

» Compare two different ecosystems, such as one that gets a lot of sunlight with one that gets less, to see whether the biotic (living) factors differ.
» Extend the project by observing the same ecosystem at different times of the year, such as in spring and in winter, and comparing the different factors.

Project extras

» Include your ecosystem drawings or photos.
» Present some of the factors you observed, such as temperature, in a table or graph.

Binoculars allow you to closely observe birds and other biotic factors in the tree tops.

What was for lunch?

Every ecosystem has a **food chain** – a process in which food energy and materials are transferred from small organisms to larger ones. Plants are **producers.** They use the energy they receive from sunlight to create their own food. Animals that are **herbivores** eat the plants. Other animals, **carnivores,** eat those animals. Other carnivores eat those animals, and so on up the chain. In this project, you will see whether you can piece together the food chain by examining what an owl ate.

Do your research

Owls are carnivores. When an owl catches its prey, it eats the entire creature, including the bones and fur. Then the owl regurgitates (brings up from its stomach) the parts of the prey its body doesn't need, in the form of a pellet. For this project, you will need to buy owl pellets from a special company. Most companies heat-sterilise the pellets, but you should still wear rubber or latex gloves and wash your hands and your work surfaces after handling the pellet. If you are allergic to fur, this project may not be safe for you.

Before you get started, learn about the food chain and food webs. You should also do some research on owls, including where they live and what animals they prey upon. Because you will be reconstructing an animal skeleton, you will need bone charts for owls' most common prey. Then you will be ready to begin the project or come up with a similar one.

Background information

Possible question

How can I study what an owl eats?

Possible hypothesis

I will be able to discover what an owl eats by studying its pellets.

Level of difficulty	Approximate cost of materials
Advanced	£15.00

Materials needed

» Newspaper
» Bone identification charts

Materials needed (cont.)

» Plastic gloves (you may be able to get some from a local delicatessen or your doctor's office)
» Two or three owl pellets (available online; search by typing "owl pellet" into a trusted search engine)
» Toothpicks
» Pieces of cardboard, each approximately 18 centimetres by 25 centimetres (7 inches by 10 inches), one for each pellet
» Fine-tipped marker
» Glue
» Large resealable plastic bags, one for each pellet, and big enough to easily fit the cardboard inside

Here are some books and websites you could start with in your research:

» *Food Chains and You*, Bobbie D Kalman (Crabtree, 2005)
» *Science Answers: Food Chains and Webs: From Producers to Decomposers*, Richard and Louise Spilsbury (Heinemann, 2004)
» RSPB: Study an owl pellet
http://www.rspb.org.uk/youth/makeanddo/do/pellet/index.asp
» The secret lives of owls: Owl pellets
http://www.carolina.com/owls/guide/pellets.asp
Follow the links at the bottom of the page to bone identification charts for each of the owl's prey.

Continued

Outline of methods

1. Cover your work area with newspaper. Lay the bone identification charts close by so you can refer to them as you work. Put on the gloves before you open the pellet.

2. Remove the pellet from its wrapper. Use both hands to carefully pull the pellet into two pieces. Some bones might be exposed. Use a toothpick to separate the bones from any fur or feathers. Clean the bones with the toothpick and your hands. Put the bones to one side.

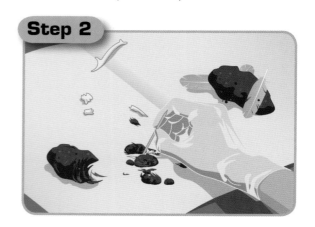

Step 2

3. Continue to pull the ball into smaller chunks and to separate the bones. After you have investigated the entire pellet, use the bone identification charts to try to determine what creature the owl ate and to identify each bone. Jawbones and skulls are usually the best clues for identifying what animal the owl ate.

4. Organise the bones on the cardboard. Use the bone identification charts to try to reconstruct the animal's skeleton. Most bones will probably be from a single animal, but you may find bones from more than one creature in a single pellet.

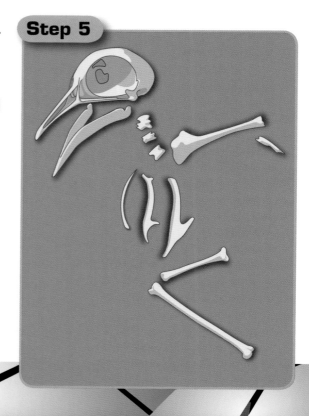

Step 5

5. Write the name of the prey on the cardboard. Glue the bones to the cardboard, labelling any ones you can identify.

6. When the glue is dry, carefully place the cardboard in the plastic bag. Make sure you seal the bag.

7. Repeat steps 2 to 6 with the other pellets.

8. When you have finished, roll the pellet remains in newspaper and throw them away. Also throw away your gloves, and then wash your hands thoroughly.

Analysis of results

» What animals' remains did you find in your pellets?
» What were some of the differences in what you found in each pellet?

More activities to extend your investigation

» If you can, order different owl species' pellets from another company, which would have collected the pellets from different locations. Compare what those owls ate with what you found in the original pellets.
» Research the eating habits of the animal whose bones you found in the owl pellet. Use this information to construct the food chain for the ecosystem in which the owl lives.
» Research and report on the special adaptations, such as night vision and excellent hearing, that make owls such effective hunters.

Project extras

» Include the cardboard with the animal bones glued to it in your report.
» Include pictures of the creatures you found in the pellets in their natural habitats.
» Include photos of an owl swooping down to attack its prey.
» Include the bone identification charts.

I'm crowded!

Have you ever seen a photo of clowns stuffed into a tiny car? It doesn't look as if it would be very comfortable. We know that people and animals need space to flourish, but do plants? In this experiment, you'll find out by planting many seeds in a small space.

Do your research

Before you get started, learn about the seeds and plants you will be using. What should they look like as they grow? How fast should they grow? You should also do some research on overcrowding of plants and **carrying capacity** – the maximum number of a species that an area can support. Once you've done your research, you may decide to vary this project or follow the directions listed here.

You could start your research using this book and these websites:

» *How Plants Survive*, Kathleen V Kudlinski (Chelsea House, 2003)
» Why plants need space too: http://www.units.muohio.edu/dragonfly/itc/one.html
» What do plants need to grow?
   http://www.kinetonprimaryschool.org.uk/kpshapegangsubjectplants.html

Background information

Possible question

Does the spacing of seeds have an effect on their growth?

Possible hypothesis

If seeds are planted too close together, they will not grow well.

Level of difficulty

Easy

Approximate cost of materials

£8.00

Materials needed

» Compass or other sharp tool
» 12 clear plastic cups
» Masking tape
» Permanent marker pen
» Potting soil, enough to fill 12 plastic cups
» 15 bean seeds
» 15 radish seeds
» 15 corn seeds
» Three plastic trays or plates, each big enough to hold four plastic cups
» Water
» Graduated cylinder or measuring jug that measures millilitres
» Ruler

Outline of methods

1. Use the compass to carefully poke a few holes in the bottom of each plastic cup.

2. Prepare three separate cups for each type of seed. Label each cup with the name of the seed and number them 1, 2, and 3. Label the three remaining cups All Seeds and number them 1, 2, and 3.

3. Fill each cup with potting soil to within 1.25 centimetres (½ inch) of the top.

Continued

4. Poke your finger about 1.25 centimetres (½ inch) into the centre of the soil. For the individual seed cups, drop one seed into the hole and cover with soil. For each of the All Seeds cups, place four of each seed in the hole and cover with soil.

5. Place the four cups labelled 1 on one of the trays. Place the cups labelled 2 and 3 on the other two trays. Put the trays in an area that gets a lot of sunlight. Wash your hands after touching the soil.

6. Water each cup just enough to moisten the soil – about 60 millilitres. Leave any water that drains through on the tray.

7. Observe the cups daily. If the soil is dry to the touch, add about 30 millilitres of water to each cup.

Step 8

8. Record the day that each seed begins to sprout, or **germinate.** Use the individual plant cups as a guide to which seeds are germinating in the All Seeds cup. Once the plants begin to grow, measure the height of each plant. Also note how many leaves it grows and record any changes in the plant's appearance.

9. Continue to record the growth of the seeds for two weeks. Compare the growth of the individual seeds with the growth of the seeds in the All Seeds cups.

Analysis of results

» Which plant in the individual cups germinated first?
» Which plant in the individual cups grew the tallest?
» Did all the seeds in each of the All Seeds cups germinate?
» Which plant in the All Seeds cups germinated first?
» Which plant in the All Seeds cups grew the tallest?
» Did any of the seeds in the All Seeds cups have unexpected or unusual growth patterns?
» Did the number of seeds affect the growth of the plants?

More activities to extend your investigation

» Show the average height of the different plant types in the All Seeds cup on your results table.
» Use different types of seeds, such as grass or flowers, and compare the results with those in the original project.
» Test how many seeds are too many. In different cups, plant varying numbers of the same type of seed in a single hole in the soil. Compare the plant growth in all of the cups.
» Plant sunflower seeds in the cup with the other seeds. Sunflowers are **allelopathic,** which means they release a chemical that prevents other plants from growing near them. Research other allelopathic plants as well.

Project extras

» Take a picture of the plants every other day. Include the photos in your report.
» Compare the growth of the single plants with the growth of the plants in the All Seeds cup in both graph and table forms.

Trapped in a greenhouse

The **atmosphere,** the layer of gases surrounding Earth, is important to life on our planet. It keeps moisture and heat "trapped" near the surface of Earth. This is called the natural **greenhouse effect.** Plants are often grown in greenhouses (above), where sunlight can enter but heat can't easily escape. To see greenhouses in action, you'll compare the growth of plants in sealed containers with that of plants grown in open containers.

Do your research

Before you start, research the greenhouse effect, how it heats Earth, and how it enables plants to grow. Also research the atmosphere and its role in the **water cycle,** the process in which Earth's water is constantly recycled. In this project, you'll observe the water cycle on a small scale in the sealed plastic bag. Once you've done your research, you'll be ready for this project or a similar one of your own.

Here are some books and websites you could start with in your research:

» *Eyewitness: Weather*, Brian Cosgrove (Dorling Kindersley, 2004)
» *Weather and Climate: Atmosphere and Weather*, Terry Jennings (Evans Brothers, 2005)
» The water cycle: http://www.bbc.co.uk/schools/riversandcoasts/water_cycle/rivers/index.shtml
» Greenhouses: http://www.greenhouses-uk.com/greenhouse_story/why.htm

Background information

Possible question

Will seeds planted in a closed container grow differently from those planted in an open container?

Possible hypothesis

Plants in a sealed container will grow faster than plants in an open container.

Level of difficulty

Easy

Approximate cost of materials

£7.50

Materials needed

» Compass or other sharp tool
» Six clear plastic cups
» Masking tape
» Permanent marker pen
» Potting soil, enough to fill six plastic cups
» Six bean seeds (dried beans sold in bags at the supermarket will work)
» Graduated cylinder or measuring jug that measures millilitres
» Water
» Three large resealable plastic freezer bags
» Two identical thermometers
» Ruler

Outline of methods

1. Use the compass to carefully poke a few holes in the bottom of each plastic cup.

2. Label three plastic cups Open and number them 1, 2, and 3. Label the other three cups Sealed and number them 1, 2, and 3.

3. Fill all six plastic cups with soil to within 1.25 centimetres (½ inch) of the top.

4. Poke your finger about 1.25 centimetres (½ inch) into the centre of the soil in each cup. Place one bean seed in each hole and cover with soil.

Continued

5. Water each cup with an equal amount of water – about 60 millilitres.

6. Put one of the cups labelled Sealed in each of the plastic bags. Place a thermometer in one of the bags. Blow in the bags to puff them out with air, and then seal the bags.

7. Place all the cups by a window where they will receive an equal amount of sunlight. Place one thermometer near the Open cups. Make sure you keep the bags out of the reach of small children and pets.

Step 7

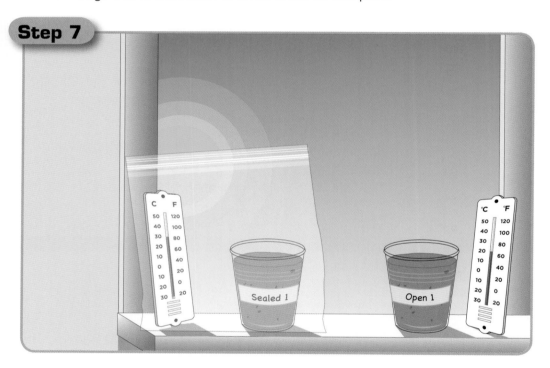

8. Observe the cups daily. Record the day that each seed germinates. Also record the temperature in the sealed bag and the room temperature near the open containers. Note how the soil in each cup looks each day.

9. Once the plants begin to grow, measure them daily; record the growth in your lab book. Measure the growth of the plants in the sealed containers from the outside of the bag. **Do not open the bags.**

10. Continue to observe plant growth for 10 days. Compare the growth of the plants in the open and sealed cups.

Analysis of results

» Did the plants in the open or sealed containers germinate first?

» Did the plants in the open or sealed containers grow taller?

» What did the soil in the open containers look like at the end of the experiment?

» What did the soil in the sealed containers look like at the end of the experiment?

More activities to extend your investigation

» Repeat the experiment with different types of seeds.

» Put all the seeds in sealed bags but vary the amount of water in each. Make sure you also record the temperature in each.

Project extras

» Include a photo or an illustration of the plants. Make sure the labels are visible.

» Show the growth results in both table and graph forms.

» Create a diagram showing how a greenhouse keeps the heat in.

Invaders!

You've probably seen weeds or other unwanted plants near your home or school. Many are plants that were brought from another area. Without natural enemies, these plants took over the space of the native plants. These intruders are called **invasives.** In this project, you will locate invasive plants around your city or town and see what effect they have on other plants.

Do your research

It is best to do this project in spring, when non-native invasive plants are most plentiful. *Non-native* refers to plants that are not originally from the area. Not all non-native plants are invasive. Some common invasive plants in the United Kingdom are Japanese knotweed and giant hogweed. Dandelions (see picture above) are invasive plants in the United States.

Before you get started, research the plants in your area. It is a good idea to speak to a plant expert at your local garden centre. He or she can help you learn about which plants are invasive and how they affect native plant life. Once you know what to look for, you can begin this project or come up with your own.

Background information

Possible question

What invasive plants are found in my town, and how do they affect the surrounding plants?

Materials needed

» Camera and film or digital camera, or drawing supplies

Possible hypothesis

Non-native invasive plants make it difficult for native species to grow.

Level of difficulty

Advanced

Approximate cost of materials

£7.00

You could start your research using this book and these websites:

» *Plant Invaders*, Dorothy Souza (Franklin Watts, 2004)

» Non-native invasive plants
http://www.plantlife.org.uk/uk/plantlife-campaigning-change-invasive-plants.html

» Invasive plants of the UK
http://www.kew.org/ksheets/pdfs/t4invasive_species.pdf

Japanese knotweed is native to Asia but is found as an invasive species throughout the United Kingdom.

Continued

Outline of methods

1. Research what plants are invasive to your area. The books and websites listed in "Do your research" will help you locate invasive species in your area. A gardening professional at your local garden centre might also be a good resource. Learn what the invasive species look like and where they are most likely to be found – such as near water, where the soil is dry, or in areas that get a lot of sunlight.

2. Walk or bike around your area to locate the invasive plants.

3. Take photos or draw pictures of the plants. After you take a picture, write the number of the photo, the plant name, and the area in which you found the plant in your lab book.

4. Also note the effect the invasives seem to have on surrounding plants, including grass. For example, how much of the area do the invasive plants cover, and do they appear to have caused the surrounding grass to die? Find areas that don't include the invasive plant; compare the condition of the plants and grass there with those in areas where the invasive is present.

Purple loosestrife originated in Europe. It is now an invasive plant in North America.

Step 3

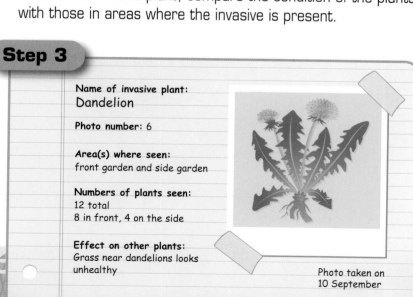

Name of invasive plant:
Dandelion

Photo number: 6

Area(s) where seen:
front garden and side garden

Numbers of plants seen:
12 total
8 in front, 4 on the side

Effect on other plants:
Grass near dandelions looks unhealthy

Photo taken on 10 September

Analysis of results

» How many different invasive plants did you find in your area?
» Which invasive plant did you see in the most places?
» Where did you find most invasive plants (near water, in sunny areas, in shady areas)?
» What effect did the invasive plants seem to have on the native plants?

More activities to extend your investigation

» Observe invasive plants over a longer time period, using a **quadrat survey.** In this type of survey, you measure two equal-size sample sections (each 1 square metre, for example) of a larger area and compare your observations in each section.
» Research common invasive plants. Find out where they originated and when they were introduced to your part of the country.
» Take the project a step further by researching animal species that are invasive in your area.

Project extras

» Include your photos or drawings of the invasive plants.
» Include a map of the area you observed and note the places where you found invasive plants.

Water cleaned with soil?

Did you know that earth is a natural filter? It might be hard to believe, but soil and rocks are natural cleaners. They help life in an ecosystem by filtering the water used by humans, animals, and plants. In this experiment, you will create your own filters and compare how well they clean dirty water.

Do your research

Before you get started, research how water is filtered through layers of sediment and ends up as **groundwater.** Groundwater is water found in underground streams between rocks and soil. You should also learn about how wetlands and other areas act as purifiers for our water. Then you'll be ready to tackle this project, or you can change the set-up to make it your own.

Here are some books and websites you could start with in your research:

» *How We Use Water*, Carol Ballard (Raintree, 2005)
» *Water: Our Precious Resource*, Roy A Gallant (Benchmark, 2003)
» What is groundwater? http://www.environment-agency.gov.uk/subjects/waterres/groundwater/106409/?version=1&lang=_e
» Earth water filter: http://www.teachersdomain.org/resources/ess05/sci/ess/earthsys/waterfilter
» Importance of wetlands: http://www.mbgnet.net/fresh/wetlands/index.htm

Background information

Possible question

Which filter will clean water the best: one with sand, polystyrene, or pebbles?

Possible hypothesis

Sand will be the best water filter.

Level of difficulty

Intermediate

Approximate cost of materials

£7.50

Materials needed

» Gardening gloves
» Potting soil

Materials needed (cont.)

» Empty 2-litre bottle, label removed
» Water
» Three empty 2-litre bottles, labels and caps removed
» Scissors
» Masking tape
» Permanent marker pen
» Four tall clear plastic cups
» Three coffee filters
» Three elastic bands
» Polystyrene pieces ("peanut-shaped" ones will work best)
» Sand
» Pebbles
» Clock or stopwatch
» Adult supervisor

Outline of methods

1. Put on the gardening gloves. Put two or three handfuls of potting soil into the first empty 2-litre bottle. Add water to fill the bottle about halfway and screw on the cap. Shake well. The bottle now holds the dirty water you will try to clean.

2. Ask an adult to cut the three empty bottles about 13 centimetres (5 inches) from the top. Discard the bottoms.

ADULT SUPERVISION REQUIRED

3. Label the three bottles Filter 1, Filter 2, and Filter 3. Do the same for three of the plastic cups.

Continued

4. Place a coffee filter over the narrow end of each bottle (the end you would normally pour from) and secure it tightly with an elastic band. This will stop the filtering material from falling out.

5. Fill the bottle labelled Filter 1 with about 8 centimetres (3 inches) of polystyrene pieces. Fill the Filter 2 bottle with an equal amount of sand and the Filter 3 bottle with the same amount of pebbles.

6. Shake the 2-litre bottle of dirty water again to make sure the water and soil are mixed. Fill the remaining plastic cup halfway with the dirty water.

7. Rest the Filter 1 bottle on top of the Filter 1 cup, so the covered end of the bottle is inside the cup. Pour the dirty water into the filter. Observe how the soil particles stick to the polystyrene. Record how long it takes for the water to completely drain into the cup. Wait until after the water has drained into the cup to remove the filter.

8. Repeat steps 6 and 7 using the Filter 2 filter and cup, and then the Filter 3 filter and cup. Make sure you use exactly the same amount of dirty water for each.

9. Compare the colours of the water in the three cups.

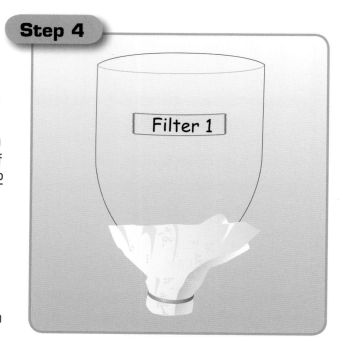

Step 4

Filter 1

Step 7

Filter 1

Filter 1

Analysis of results

» Which filter worked best?

» Which worked worst?

» Which filter did it take the dirty water longest to filter through?

More activities to extend your investigation

» Research how pollution from people and factories affects the natural filtration process.

» Create a single filter with even layers of each material. After the dirty water drains through the filter, take it apart and try to determine which layer did most of the "cleaning".

» Expand the project to test how well other materials, such as cotton wool balls, filter dirty water.

Project extras

» Include "before" and "after" photos or drawings of each filtering material. Also include photos or drawings of the dirty water before and after it passed through each filter.

» Create a poster of your project. Decorate the borders with some unused pieces of polystyrene.

The disappearing apple

When a tree dies in the forest, where does it go? Over time, it begins to disappear. We can thank **decomposers** for this. Decomposers, such as worms, termites, fungi, and microorganisms, feed on dead plant and animal matter. This matter eventually becomes part of the soil. How much do decomposers affect an ecosystem? In this experiment, you'll compare how quickly apples decompose with and without an added decomposer.

Do your research

Before you start, find out more about decomposers and the role they play in an ecosystem. Also research the fungus yeast, which you'll use as a decomposer in this experiment. After you have done your research, you will be ready to do the experiment or one similar to it. During this experiment, make sure you keep the sealed bags out of the reach of small children. The bags should be clearly marked as part of your experiment. Eating rotten apples covered in yeast is dangerous and can make people very sick!

Background information

Possible question

Will yeast make an apple decompose faster than it normally would?

Possible hypothesis

A fungus, such as yeast, will cause an apple to decompose faster than it normally would.

Level of difficulty

Easy

Approximate cost of materials

£2.50

Materials needed

» Eight small resealable plastic bags
» Permanent marker pen
» Two fresh apples
» Knife (make sure you get permission to cut the apple or ask an adult to cut it for you)
» One fresh packet of active dry yeast
» Measuring spoon
» Camera and film or digital camera

Here are some books and websites you could start with in your research:

» *Decomposers in the Food Chain*, Alice B McGinty (Rosen Publishing, 2002)
» *Food Chains and Webs: From Producers to Decomposers*, Richard and Louise Spilsbury (Heinemann, 2004)
» What is a decomposer?
http://www.nhptv.org/natureworks/nwep11b.htm
» RSPB: Decomposers
http://www.rspb.org.uk/youth/learn/foodchains/decomposers.asp

Outline of methods

1. Label four of the plastic bags Yeast and the other four No Yeast.
2. Cut the apples into four equal pieces.
3. Place one apple slice in each bag.

Continued

4. Measure 5 millilitres (1 teaspoon) of yeast. Pour the yeast onto the white part of the apple slices in the four Yeast bags. Seal the bags.

5. Without adding any yeast, seal the No Yeast bags.

6. Take photos of each bag. Make sure you keep the bags out of the reach of small children and pets.

7. Observe the apples each day. In your research journal, note any changes you see. Take photos or make drawings of each apple every two days.

8. Continue to observe the apples for at least one week. Compare how quickly the apples in the bags decompose.

9. When you complete the experiment, throw the sealed bags with the apples in them into the bin.

Step 8

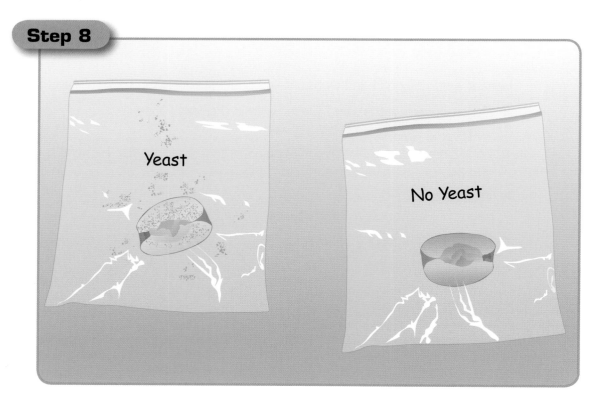

Yeast

No Yeast

Analysis of results

» Which apples decomposed the fastest?

» What types of changes occurred?

More activities to extend your investigation

» Vary the amount of yeast on additional apple slices and compare the results to those in the original project.

» Test whether different types of apples decompose faster than others. Or test whether apples of the same type decompose faster if one is ripe and one is not.

» Do the experiment with foods other than apples, such as bananas or potatoes, and compare the results.

Project extras

» Include the photos you took of each of the apple slices during the experiment.

» Include pictures of decomposers, such as mushrooms growing on a rotten log or vultures flying over a carcass.

The apples in this box decomposed at different rates. What factors might have been involved?

Puddle and pond pH

Ecosystems are made up of different sources of water – some contain salt and some are fresh water. One other key difference is the **acidity** of different bodies of water. The acidity of the water source affects all life that uses the water. In this experiment, you will compare the **pH** of different bodies of water in your town, such as tap water, rainwater, ponds, puddles, and lakes.

Do your research

In this project, you'll test the acidity of different water sources using pH paper. Make sure you choose safe bodies of water to test; wear gloves if necessary. Avoid putting yourself in a dangerous position as you collect water samples. An adult should accompany you to gather samples from sources in nature, such as ponds or lakes. It's best to start this project before a rain shower so you can later collect and test rainwater and puddles. Find out more about the pH scale and how pH paper works. Also learn more about acids and bases. Afterwards, you'll be ready to try this experiment, or you may want to create your own.

Background information

Possible question

Is the pH of all water sources in an ecosystem the same?

Possible hypothesis

The pH of water can vary depending on the source.

Level of difficulty

Intermediate

Approximate cost of materials

£7.50

Materials needed

» Empty film canisters, jars, or other containers to collect water
» Masking tape
» Permanent marker pen
» pH paper strips (may be available from your science teacher or from aquarium supply shops, or you can order them online; type "pH paper strips" into a trusted search engine.)
» Adult supervisor

Here are some books and websites you could start with in your research:

» *Material Matters: Acids and Bases*, Carol Baldwin (Raintree, 2004)
» *How We Use Water*, Carol Ballard (Raintree, 2005)
» *Water: Our Precious Resource*, Roy A Gallant (Benchmark, 2003)
» Kids' corner: pH scale
http://www.ec.gc.ca/acidrain/kids.html
» Water pollution and testing
http://fi.edu/guide/bond/pollution.html
» UK Environment Agency: Acid rain
http://www.environment-agency.gov.uk/yourenv/eff/1190084/pollution/acid_rain/

Continued

Outline of methods

1. Fill one container with tap water. Label the container.

2. Decide what bodies of water you are going to test, such as a lake, a puddle, and a pond. Label the containers with the names of the water sources you will test. Use at least one container to collect rainwater.

3. **An adult should accompany you as you collect samples from the bodies of water you will be testing.**

4. Follow the directions on the container for using the pH paper strips. They should instruct you to dip one end of a strip into one of your water samples. Wait for the strip to change colour, and then compare your strip to the colour key provided with the paper. Repeat for the remaining water samples. Make sure you wash your hands after handling the pH paper.

5. Record the pH of each body of water in a chart. Compare the pH levels of the water samples.

Step 4

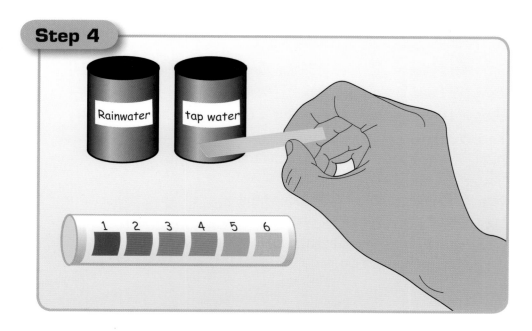

Analysis of results

» Which water sample was the most acidic (closest to 0)?

» Were any samples **alkaline** – above 7 on the pH scale?

» Which two bodies of water were the closest in pH?

» What factors may have had an effect on the pH of certain samples, such as the one taken from a puddle?

More activities to extend your investigation

» Compare the pH levels of rainwater taken from the same location on different days.

» Research the ways acid rain and pollution can affect the pH level of bodies of water and the organisms that live there.

Project extras

» Include photos of each body of water you tested.

» Use crayons or markers to create a chart that shows the colours your pH paper turned for each sample.

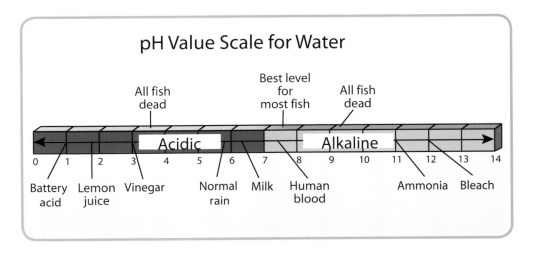

pH Value Scale for Water

No good water

In the previous project ("Puddle and pond pH"), you learned about how the pH level is different in various water sources. Pollutants can change the pH level of rain to make it more acidic. Acid rain can cause damage to statues and buildings and can also destroy forests and plant life. In this experiment, you will test the effect that high levels of an acid have on plants.

Do your research

In this project, you will water plants with different combinations of vinegar. Because vinegar is an acid, make sure you wash your hands after doing the experiment. Before you begin, research the causes of acid rain and how it affects plants, animals, and even buildings and statues. You will also need a good understanding of the pH scale. After learning about acid rain and pH, you'll be ready to begin this project – or you may come up with your own.

Here are some books and websites you could start with in your research:

» *Water: Our Precious Resource*, Roy A Gallant (Benchmark, 2003)
» *How Plants Survive*, Kathleen V Kudlinski (Chelsea House, 2003)
» Acid rain and pH
   http://www.epa.gov/acidrain/education/site_students/phscale.html

Background information

Possible question

Will acid have an effect on plant growth?

Possible hypothesis

Acid will cause the plants to grow more slowly.

Level of difficulty

Intermediate

Approximate cost of materials

£7.00

Materials needed

» Compass or other sharp tool
» Nine clear plastic cups
» Masking tape
» Permanent marker pen
» Potting soil
» Bean seeds (dried beans sold in bags at the supermarket will work)
» Three plastic plates or trays, each big enough to hold three plastic cups
» Water
» Graduated cylinder or measuring jug that measures millilitres
» Vinegar
» Ruler

» What is acid rain?
http://www.yptenc.org.uk/docs/factsheets/env_facts/acid_rain.html
» Kids' corner: pH scale: http://www.ec.gc.ca/acidrain/kids.html

Outline of methods

1. Use the compass to carefully poke a few holes in the bottom of each cup. Label three cups Water 1, Water 2, and Water 3. Label three cups 50% Vinegar 1, 50% Vinegar 2, and 50% Vinegar 3. Label the last three cups 100% Vinegar 1, 100% Vinegar 2, and 100% Vinegar 3.

2. Fill each cup with soil to within about 1.25 centimetres (½ inch) of the top.

Continued

3. Poke your finger about 1.25 centimetres (½ inch) into the centre of the soil. Place three seeds in each hole and cover with soil.

4. Place one group of cups on each tray. Place the trays by a window where all the cups will receive an equal amount of sunlight.

5. Water each cup just enough to moisten the soil – about 60 millilitres. Leave any water that drains through on the tray.

6. Observe the cups every other day. Record the day each seed germinates and measure and record each seed's growth in your lab book. If the soil is dry to the touch, add about 30 millilitres of water to each cup.

7. Once the plants are at least 2.5 centimetres (1 inch) tall – after about one week – water each cup with the appropriate liquid. Add 50 millilitres of water to the cups labelled Water. For the 50% Vinegar cups, mix 25 millilitres of vinegar with 25 millilitres of water and pour into the cups. Add 50 millilitres of vinegar to the cups labelled 100% Vinegar. Make sure you keep the vinegar out of the reach of small children and pets.

8. Continue to record the height of each plant in your lab book. Include a description of what the soil looks like each day and draw pictures of the plants as they change.

9. Continue to water the plants as needed (when the soil feels dry to the touch) with the same amount of the liquids from step 7.

10. Continue to record the growth of the plants for two more weeks. Compare the growth of the plants in the cups.

Step 7

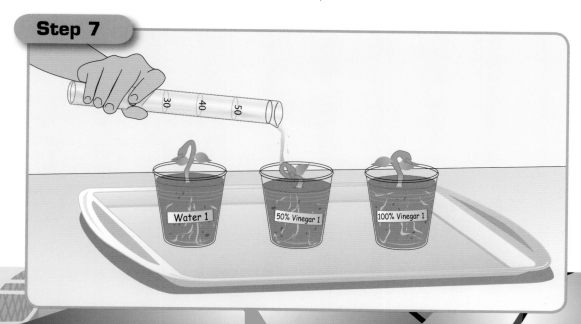

Analysis of results

» Which plant grew the tallest?
» What changes did you notice in the plants after you added the vinegar?
» Did you notice any changes to the soil?

More activities to extend your investigation

» Repeat the experiment using other common natural acids, such as lemon juice and orange juice, and compare the results.
» Test plants that grow better in acidic soils, such as azaleas and rhododendrons, with ones that grow better in neutral soils. Re-pot the plants so they are all in the same type of soil.
» Try the experiment without soil. Instead, plant the beans in cotton wool. This allows you to test whether the acid is the problem, or whether it is toxic substances released from the soil by the acid that is the problem.
» Try the experiment with water plants, such as duckweed. You can buy this from aquarium suppliers. Compare the water plant results with the soil plant results.

Project extras

» Take a picture of the plants every other day and include the photos in your report.
» Create a line or bar graph of the plants' growth.

Writing your report

In many ways, writing the report of your investigation is the hardest part. You've researched the science involved, and you've had fun gathering all your evidence together. Now you have to explain what it's all about.

You are the expert

Very few other people, if any, will have done your investigation. So you are the expert here. You need to explain your ideas clearly. Scientists get their most important investigations published in a scientific magazine or journal. They may also stand up at meetings and tell other scientists what they have found. Or they may display a large poster to explain their investigation. You might consider giving a talk or making a poster about your investigation, too. But however scientists present their investigations, they always write it down first – and you must too. Here are some tips about what you should include in your report.

Some hints for collecting your results

» **Making a table:** Tables are great for recording lots of results. Use a pencil and ruler to draw your table lines, or make a table using a word processing program. Put the units (m, s, kg, N and so on) in the headings only. Don't write them into the main body of your table. Try to make your table fit one side of paper. If you need two sheets of paper, make sure you write the column headings on the second sheet as well.

» **Recording your results:** It is often easy to forget to write down your results as they come in. Or you might just scribble them onto the back of your hand, and then wash your hands! A wise scientist will always make a neat, blank table in their lab book before starting. They will write down their results as they go along and not later on.

» **Odd stuff:** If something goes wrong, make a note of it. This will remind you which results might not be reliable.

» **Precision:** Always record your readings to the precision of your measuring equipment. For example, if you have scales that show 24.6 g, don't write 24 or 25 in your table. Instead, write 24.6 because that's the precise measurement.

Laying out your report

You could use the following headings to organise your report in a clear manner:

» A title
This gives an idea of what your investigation is about.

» Aims
Write a brief outline of what you were trying to do. It should include the question you were trying to answer.

» Hypothesis
This is your scientific prediction of what will happen in your investigation. Include notes from your research to explain why you think your prediction will work out. It might help to write it out as: "I think ... will happen because ..."

» Materials
List the equipment you used to carry out your experiments. Also say what any measuring equipment was for. For example, "scales (to weigh the objects)".

» Methods
Explain what you actually did in your investigation.

» Results
Record your results, readings, and observations clearly.

» Conclusions
Explain how closely your results fitted your hypothesis. You can find out more about this on the next page.

» Bibliography
List the books, articles, websites or other resources you used in your research.

And finally ... the conclusions

There are two main bits to your conclusions. These are the "Analysis" and the "Evaluation". In the analysis you explain what your evidence shows, and how it supports or disproves your hypothesis. In the evaluation, you discuss the quality of your results and their reliability, and how successful your methods were.

Your analysis

You need to study your evidence to see if there is a relationship between the variables in your investigation. This can be difficult to spot in a table, so it is a good idea to draw a graph. You should always put the dependent variable on the vertical axis, and the independent variable on the horizontal axis. The type of graph you need to draw depends on the type of variables involved:

» A bar chart if the results are **categoric**, such as hot/cold, male/female.
» A line graph or a scattergram if both variables are **continuous**, such as time, length, or mass.

Remember to label the axes to say what each one shows, and the unit used. For example, "time in s" or "height in cm". Draw a line or curve of best fit if you can.

Explain what your graph shows. Remember that the reader needs help from you to understand your investigation. Even if you have spotted a pattern, don't assume that your reader has. Tell them. For example, "My graph shows that the more acid added, the slower the growth of the plant". Circle any points on your graph that seem anomalous (too high or too low).

Your evaluation

Did your investigation go well, or did it go badly? Was your evidence good enough for you to support or disprove your hypothesis? Sometimes it can be difficult for you to answer these questions. But it is really important that you try. Scientists always look back at their investigations. They want to know if they could improve their methods next time. They also want to know if their evidence is reliable and valid. Reliable evidence can be repeated with pretty much the same results. Valid evidence is reliable, and it should answer the question you asked in the first place. As before, remember that you are the person who knows your investigation the best. Don't be afraid to show off valid evidence. And be honest if it's not!

Glossary

abiotic non-living

acidity amount of acid in a substance

alkaline describes a compound with a pH above 7

allelopathic able to release chemicals that kill surrounding plants

atmosphere layer of gases that surrounds Earth

biotic living

carnivore animal that eats meat

carrying capacity maximum number of a given species that an area can support

categoric variable that can be given labels, such as male/female

continuous variable that can have any value, such as weight or length

control something that is left unchanged in order to compare results against it

data factual information

decomposer organism that breaks down dead plants or animals

evidence data that has been checked to see if it is valid

food chain system in which energy is passed from plants to animals

germinate begin to grow; sprout

greenhouse effect warming of Earth's surface caused by heat and moisture trapped by the atmosphere

groundwater underground water that feeds wells and springs

herbivore animal that eats plants

hypothesis scientific idea about how something works, before the idea has been tested

invasives plants or animals that are not native to an area

pH measure of whether a substance is an acid or a base

producer organism that can make its own food

prediction say in advance what you think will happen

quadrat survey scientific study in which conditions within two or more equal-size sample sections of a larger area are compared

variable something that can change; is not set or fixed

water cycle continuous cycle in which water moves from Earth to the atmosphere and back again

Index